SHE!

ROBERT A. JOHNSON

SHE!

A contribution to understanding
feminine psychology,
Based on the myth of Amor and Psyche,
And using Jungian psychological concepts.

by
Robert A. Johnson

Religious Publishing Company
198 Allendale Road
King of Prussia, Pa. 19406
1976

To John Sanford
Certainly the Godfather
of this work.

Acknowledgments

My great appreciation to Glenda Taylor and Helen Macey for the heroic tasks of transcriptions, additions, editing and typing the lecture tapes into readable form. My gratitude to the many people of the Parish of St. Paul in San Diego for their contributions to the evolution of this book.

SHE!

Table of Contents

Introduction

The story of *Amor and Psyche* is one of the best elucidations one could find of the psychology of the feminine personality. It is an ancient, pre-Christian myth, first recorded in classical Greek times, having had a long oral tradition before that; yet it is still pertinent to us today.

That it should be so is not strange for, as the chemistry of the human body is the same today as it was in Greek times, so also the unconscious psychological dynamic of human personality is the same. Basic human needs, both physical and psychological, remain fixed, although the form in which they are satisfied may vary from time to time.

This is why when we want to study the

basic patterns of human behavior and personality, it is instructive to go to the earliest sources where their portrayal is apt to be so direct and so simple we cannot fail to see them. Then perhaps, if we can understand the basic structure, we can begin to see the changes and variations peculiar to our own time.

Myths are rich sources of psychological insight. Great literature, as with all great art, records and portrays the human condition with indelible accuracy. Myths are a special kind of literature. They are usually not written or created by a single individual, but are the product of the collective imagination and experience of an entire age and culture. Myths seem to develop gradually as certain motifs emerge, are elaborated, and finally are rounded out as people tell and retell certain stories that catch and hold their interest. Thus themes that are accurate and universal are kept alive, while those elements peculiar to single individuals usually drop away. Myths, therefore, portray a collective image. They tell about things that are true for all men.

This belies our current rationalistic society's definition of myth as something untrue or imaginary. "Why, that's a myth; it's not true at all," we hear. But actually, for the reasons suggested above, a myth is profoundly and universally true.

A myth may be a fantasy; it may be a product of the imagination, but it is nonetheless true and real. It depicts levels of reality that include the outer rational world as well as the less understood inner world within the psyche of each individual.

This confusion concerning the narrow definition of reality may be illustrated by the thinking of a small child after a nightmare. A parent may say, to be comforting, "It was only a dream; the monster was not real." But the child is unconvinced, and rightly so. To him it was real, as alive and real as any outer experience. The monster he dreamed about was in his head and not in his bedroom, but it had, nonetheless, an awesome reality, with power over the child's emotional and physical reactions. It had an inner reality for him that cannot and should not be denied.

A myth is a product of the collective imagination and not of scientific or rational development, but it is profoundly real. Because of its manner of development, through years of retelling and refining by countless people, it carries a powerful collective meaning.

Myths have been carefully studied by many psychologists. C. G. Jung, for example, in his studies of the underlying structure of the human personality, paid particular attention to myths. He found in them an expression of basic psychological patterns. We may hope to do the same with our study of *Amor and Psyche.*

But first we must learn to think mythologically, a delightful and thrilling process. Powerful things happen when we touch the mythological thinking which myths, fairy tales and our own dreams bring to us. The terms and settings of the old myths are strange; they seem archaic and distant to us, but if we listen to them carefully and take them seriously, we begin to hear and to understand. Sometimes it is necessary to translate a symbolic meaning, but this is not difficult once we see how it can be done.

Many psychologists who have read *Amor and Psyche* have interpreted it as a statement of the feminine personality. Perhaps it would be wise at the very beginning of this study to say that we are speaking of femininity wherever it is found, in men as well as in women.

Dr. Jung, in one of his most profound insights, showed that, just as genetically every man has recessive female chromosomes and hormones, so too every man has a group of feminine psychological characteristics that make up a minority element within him. A woman likewise has a psychological masculine minority component within her. The man's feminine side Dr. Jung called the anima; the woman's masculine side he called the animus.

Much has been written about the anima and the animus and we will have more to say about both of them later. At this point, suffice it to say that whenever we speak of the feminine aspects of the Amor and Psyche myth, we are speaking not only about women, but also about the man's anima, his feminine side. The connection may be more obvious to a woman, since femininity is her major psychological quality, yet there will also be something of a parallel to a man's anima.

1

et us begin then with our story of *Amor and Psyche.* It seems that there was a kingdom. There is always a kingdom; that is the beginning of everything. There is a king and a queen, and they have three daughters. The two eldest daughters are ordinary princesses (if a princess can be ordinary); they are not very remarkable.

The third daughter, who is named Psyche, is an extraordinary person. She is beautiful, charming, so like a goddess in her bearing, her speech and her whole personality that a cult of worship has sprung up around her. People have begun to say, "Here is the new Aphrodite. Here is a new goddess."

Now Aphrodite was an age-old goddess of femininity who had reigned since the beginning; no one knew just how long. But people began saying that Psyche was taking her place. In the poetic and beautiful terms of the myth, the ashes of the sacramental fires in the temple of Aphrodite grew cold.

The origins of these two, Aphrodite and Psyche, are interesting. When the genitals of Uranus were severed and fell into the sea, the sea was fertilized and Aphrodite was born. This birth was immortalized in a magnificent painting by Botticelli, called the Birth of Venus. Venus is the Roman name for Aphrodite. The painting depicts Venus being borne in upon a wave, standing on a shell; it is an exquisitely beautiful thing. On the other hand, it was rumored that Psyche was born when dewdrops from the sky fell upon the land. Here we begin our mythological unraveling.

The difference between these two births, if properly understood, reveals the different natures of these two goddesses. Aphrodite is a goddess born out of the sea; she is primeval, oceanic femininity. She is of a preconscious evolutionary time; she is at home at the bottom of the sea and holds court there. As Eric Neumann has said, she is the goddess of swamp fertility. In psychological terms, she reigns in the unconscious, symbolized by the waters of the sea. She is therefore scarcely approachable on normal conscious human terms. One can hardly cope with oceanic femininity; one might as well argue with a tidal wave. It is difficult to touch or come to terms with the Aphrodite nature, as it is primitive femininity. One can admire or worship or be crushed by it, or one can go the way of this myth, Psyche's way of evolving to a new level of femininity. Those are the choices.

Every woman has an Aphrodite in her who is easily recognized, her chief characteristics being vanity, conniving lust, fertility, and tyranny when she is crossed.

There are marvelous stories about Aphrodite and her court. She has a servant who carries a mirror before her so that she may admire herself. Someone continually makes perfume for her. She is jealous and will stand no competition whatsoever. She is constantly arranging marriages and is never satisfied until everyone is busily serving her fertility. Women who are matchmakers, and are not satisfied if any bachelor is left loose, are Aphrodites.

Actually, one sees Aphrodite everywhere. At every supermarket, Aphrodite parks her grocery cart squarely in the middle of the aisle and says, "If you won't court me, you will at least bump into me." That is Aphrodite.

It is very embarrassing for a modern, reasonably intelligent woman to discover her own Aphrodite nature and all of the primitive, instinctive tricks she plays. There are women who get into a rage if their husbands deviate so much as an inch from the straight and narrow line they have dictated. This is Aph-

12

rodite.

Naturally, when a new kind of femininity appears on the stage of evolution, Aphrodite, goddess of the old femininity, is going to be irate. For she is absolutely beyond any morality; she is before the time of morality. She will use any means at her disposal to down an opponent. She is, in fact, a thorough bitch. Every woman knows this through her own sudden regressions to her Aphrodite nature, for a woman is a terrifying figure when she falls into it. Every male around her trembles, for men are terrified of Aphrodite. It is a calmer household where someone can gently say, "Now look, sweet, remember Aphrodite?"

Yet Aphrodite is a valuable person. She is that basic, instinctive motherhood necessary for reproduction of the species. As time goes on, we will see that she does not crush Psyche; on the contrary, she does all that is right to make Psyche grow, though she is so unpleasant about it one does not feel like giving her a great deal of credit.

One of the beautiful things about the structure of the unconscious in human personality is that when it is time for growth, the old ways, the old habits pave the way and welcome the new. They *seem* to persecute the new growth at every point, but who knows—perhaps that is the correct way to bring a new consciousness to birth.

There is a story about the first elephant born in captivity. At first its keeper was delighted, but then he was horrified when the other elephants in the compound gathered in a circle and tossed the baby to each other. The keeper thought they were killing it, but they were only making it breathe.

Often, when new growth occurs, the most dreadful things seem to happen, but then one sees that they were exactly what was required. Aphrodite, who is criticized at every turn, does everything to make Psyche's evolution possible. One can be optimistic after the fact, but it is devilishly painful while it is happening. There is a sort of chaotic evolutionary warfare within one during this time. The old way, the Aphrodite nature in this case, is regressive, pulling one back into unconsciousness, yet at the same time forcing one forward into new life, sometimes at great risk. It may be that evolution could be accomplished in another way; it may be that at times Aphrodite is the only element that can bring about growth. There are women, for example, who would not grow unless they had a tyrant of a mother-in-law. (Aphrodite turns up regularly in mothers-in-law. The wicked stepmother is also a parallel.)

Most of the turmoil for a modern woman is the collision between her Aphrodite nature and her Psyche nature. It may help her to have a framework for understanding the process because, if she can see what is happening, she is already well on her way to a new consciousness. Recognizing Aphrodite can be of great value to her. When a man can recognize Aphrodite in a woman, and know what to do or what not to do, he is well off.

14

2

Now that we have learned something of the nature of Aphrodite, the older, more primitive level of femininity, let us look at the new arrival on the scene, Psyche. Psyche was born when a dewdrop fell on the land. The land is the symbol for consciousness, so we see a change from the ocean to the land. Instead of oceanic proportions of unconsciousness, we have the manageable waters of a dewdrop.

Psyche's nature is so magnificent, so unworldly, so virginal and pure that she is worshipped, *but she is not courted.* This is an utterly lonely experience and poor Psyche finds no husband.

In this sense, there is a Psyche in every woman, and it is intensely lonely. Every woman is, in part, a king's daughter, too lovely, too perfect, too deep for the ordinary world. When a woman finds herself lonely and not understood, when she finds that people are good to her but stay just a little distance away, she has found the Psyche nature in her own person. It is terribly painful. Women are often excruciatingly aware of this without knowing its origin, which is the Psyche nature, and there is nothing that can be done about it. That part of one will remain untouched, unrelated, unmarried most of one's life.

All manner of nonsense goes on when a woman tries to bring her Psyche nature into the everyday give and take of a relationship. If the Psyche nature is a large part of a woman, she has a painful task on her hands. She bursts into tears and says, "But nobody understands." And it is true; nobody understands. Every woman has this quality within her; it makes no difference what her station in life may be. If one knows of this quality and can touch it in a woman, the great beauty of a Psyche can be made conscious in her and a noble evolution may begin.

If a woman is very beautiful, the problem is compounded. Marilyn Monroe is a good example. She was worshipped far and wide, yet she never succeeded in relating closely to anyone. Finally she found it intolerable. Such a person seems to be the carrier of a goddess-like quality, an almost unapproachable perfection. If one understands, perhaps one can set in motion the evolution which was required of Psyche, but it is not easy.

I once saw a film in which two horribly disfigured people in an institution fell in love with each other. Through the magic of fantasy they made each infinitely beautiful to the other, and a love affair went on between these two handsome, beautiful people. At the end of the movie, the camera blurred back to show the two originally disfigured faces, but the audience knew where they had been; they had seen the god and goddess within.

Psyche is the distress of her parents because, while her two older sisters are married happily to neighboring kings, no one asks for Psyche's hand. They only worship her. The king goes to an oracle, who happens to be dominated by Aphrodite, and she, irate and jealous of Psyche, has the oracle give a terrible prophesy that Psyche is to be married to Death, the ugliest, the most horrible, the most awful creature possible. Psyche is to be taken to the top of a mountain, chained to a rock, and left to be ravished by this dreadful creature, Death.

Oracles were received without recourse in Greek society; they were absolute truth. So Psyche's parents don't question this decision. They make a wedding procession, which is a funeral cortege, take Psyche as instructed, and chain her to the rock at the top of the mountain. There are floods of tears; wedding finery and funeral darkness are mixed together. Then the parents extinguish the torches and leave Psyche alone in the dark.

What can we make of this? Psyche is to be married. Her husband will come, but this is an unhappy occasion because her husband is Death itself. The maiden dies on her wedding day; her wedding is a funeral. But this is instructive. Many of our wedding customs are actually funeral customs. In primitive weddings, marriage was celebrated as such; it was at once a funeral, a transformation, and a joyous outburst. Many of our customs stem from primitive times when weddings were abductions and the best man and his friends were abductors. The bridesmaids were protectors of the virginity of the bride. If a man could not win a woman in this way, he was not worthy of her. Funeral rites and abduction ceremonies are still present in our weddings. One is not inclined to remind people of this on wedding days, but many a bride cries on her wedding day. Instinctively she knows that the maiden in her is dying.

One of the problems with marriage is that we no longer recognize or observe this duality in custom or ritual, and all manner of trouble comes from this fact. But the dual impact of marriage is simply inescapable. It is as much ours as it was the ancient Greeks, yet it is ignored. We do not have a place for the girl's dying experience in the wedding. We try to make it all happy and white and pink and joyous, but somewhere we should reckon with the dying part. If we do not, that component will have to be 'lived out' at a later, perhaps less appropriate time. This is generally experienced by the woman as a fierce resentment against her marriage.

I have seen a picture of a Turkish wedding party in which boys of eight or nine each had one foot bound to his thigh and was hopping on one leg. This was to remind everyone that pain was present at the wedding as well as joy.

In African weddings, unless the bride arrives with scars and wounds evident on her, it is not a valid wedding. We would call that barbaric, and it is, but elemental reality had best be observed somewhere along the way. Perhaps the girl who comes to her mother a few hours before the wedding and bursts into tears is wise. For if the sacrificial element of a wedding is given its due, the joy of the marriage is possible. Aphrodite does not like maidens to die at the hands of men. It is not her nature to be subject to a man. So the Aphrodite in a woman is either crying or fuming, or both, at her wedding.

Here again we observe the paradox of evolution mentioned earlier. It is Aphrodite who condemns Psyche to death but who is also the matchmaker who brings about weddings in the first place. Yet Aphrodite also weeps and rages at the wedding for the possible loss of the bride's freedom and individuality, for the loss of her virginity. The forward push of evolution toward marriage is accompanied by a regressive tug of longing for the autonomy and freedom of things as they were before.

A wedding is a powerful time. All manner of elemental forces are loose. I once saw a cartoon that summed up the archetypal power of a wedding with great genius. It showed the thoughts of each of the parents. The father of the bride is angry at that fellow who is audacious enough to snatch his darling away from him; the father of the groom is triumphant at the supremacy of the males of the community, for a day at least; the mother of the bride is horrified at the beast who is intruding; the mother of the groom is horrified at the creature who has seduced her pure son away from her. All of the archetypes (those ancient, embedded patterns of thought and behavior laid down in the unconscious of the human psyche through countless years of evolution) were loose in the cartoon.

3

I n order to destroy Psyche, as she wishes to do, Aphrodite has to have help, and she engages the assistance of her son, Eros, the god of love. Eros, Amor and Cupid are various names which have been given to the god of love. Since Cupid has been degraded to the level of valentine cards, and Amor has been shorn of his dignity, let us use the name Eros for this noble god.

Eros carries his quiver of arrows and is the bane of everyone on Olympus; not even Zeus himself escapes the power of Eros. Yet Eros is under his mother's thumb. Aphrodite instructs him to enflame Psyche with love for the loathsome beast who will come to claim her, thus ending Psyche's challenge to Aphrodite. One of Aphrodite's characteristics is that she is constantly regressive. She wants things to go back where they were; she wants evolution to go backward. She is the voice of tradition, and ironically it is a beautiful voice when intelligently used.

There are many levels from which to view Eros. He may be seen as the outer man, the husband or the male in every relationship; or he may be seen as the woman's animus, her own inner masculinity. We will speak to both of these aspects of Eros in our myth as we continue.

Eros goes to do his mother's bidding, but just as he glimpses Psyche, he accidentally pricks his finger on one of his own arrows, and falls in love with her. He decides on the spot to take Psyche as his own bride, and asks his friend, the West Wind, to lift her very gently down from the top of the mountain into the Valley of Paradise. The West Wind does this, and Psyche, who was expecting the worst, finds herself in a heaven on earth instead. She does not ask Eros any questions. Imagine landing in an alabaster hall with servants, music, fine food, entertainment and beauty all day long! Of course she doesn't ask any questions. It has been enough to be delivered from facing death; she does not want or need any more consciousness now. Sometimes one feels that there has been enough of evolution for the present, and asks nothing more.

The experience of Psyche on the death

mountain is a strange thing. There are women of fifty who have never been to the death mountain, though they may be grandmothers. The dewy quality is not off the world for them even in middle age. There are also young girls of sixteen who know all about that experience, have been through it and survived it, and have a terrifying wisdom in their eyes.

These things do not happen automatically at any age. I knew a girl of sixteen who had a baby out of season. She went off to have it privately and quietly, and the baby was adopted. She never saw it. She came back and nothing had happened to that girl; she had not learned a thing. Several years later she was married, and if anybody could be called virgin, she could. Psychologically she had not been touched, even though she had had a baby.

So the Psyche in each woman terminates her naivety at vastly different times in life; it is not just when she marries. Many girls are through it by sixteen, which is bitter; one should not be chained on the mountain at sixteen.

Marriage is a totally different thing to a man than to a woman. The man is adding to his stature; his world is getting stronger, and he has come up a peg. He generally does not understand that he is killing the Psyche in his newfound wife, and that he has to. If she behaves strangely, or collapses, or if something goes dreadfully wrong, he usually doesn't understand that marriage is a totally different experience for her than for him.

Anyway, our Psyche of the myth finds that her paradise is magnificent. She has everything one could wish. Her god-husband Eros is with her every night. He puts only one restriction on her: he extracts from her the promise that she will not look at him and will not inquire into any of his ways. She may have anything she wishes, she may live in her paradise, but she must not ask to know him. Psyche agrees to this. She wants to be his wife and to do whatever he wishes.

Nearly every man wants this of his wife. If she will just not ask for consciousness; if she will just do things his way. He wants the old patriarchal marriage where the man decides all the important issues, the woman says yes to him, and there is no trouble. Every man harbors within him the hope that this is how it will be, and for a little while there is the possibility that marriage will go forward in this way.

For some reason, the Psyche in every woman has to go through a stage, at least briefly, in which she is totally subject to a man. It is an archetypal level that cannot be avoided. A woman need not stay there long, but she must have the experience briefly. This may be an echo of some primitive patriarchal practice in which she is subject to the man. There are remnants of the patriarchal world in our customs, such as the woman's bearing the man's name. Psyche goes through such a patriarchal experience. Eros insists that she not ask any questions, she agrees, and they are content in paradise.

Every immature Eros is a paradise

maker. It is adolescent to carry a girl off and promise her that she will live happily ever after. That is Eros in a secretive stage; he wants his paradise, but no responsibility, no conscious relationship. There is a bit of this in every man. The feminine demand for evolution—and most evolution comes from the feminine element in the myths, either from the woman or the anima—is a terrifying thing to a man. He would like it just to be a paradise. But all paradises are suspect; they just do not work well. It is Eros' childishness or boyishness (Eros is pure Puer Eternis) that makes this demand.

Listen to lovers build a paradise. It is such fun and so beautiful. Someone listening to such people could say, "Look, it isn't going to go like that at all." But they wouldn't listen; they are in paradise.

There is something in the unconscious of a man that wishes to make an agreement with his wife that she shall ask no questions of him. A man's attitude toward marriage is that it should be there for him to come home to, but should not be an encumbrance; he wants to be free to forget about it when he wants to focus elsewhere. This is a great shock to a woman when she discovers it. Marriage is a total commitment for a woman; for a man this is not so. I remember a woman who told me she cried for days when she discovered that their marriage was merely a detail in her husband's life, though it was her whole life. She had discovered her husband in his Eros, paradise-making nature.

4

All paradises fail; each one has a serpent of some kind in it. That is the nature of paradise; it demands that its opposite shall appear quickly. Our own Christian paradise of Eden had a serpent in it. Psyche's paradise had its awakening element in it also.

It seems that Psyche's two sisters, who had been mourning her loss—though not vigorously, it had been noticed—hear that Psyche is living in a garden paradise and that she has a god as a husband. Their jealousy knows no bounds. They come to the crag where Psyche had been chained and call down to her in the garden. They send the best of wishes and inquiries about her health.

Psyche naively reports all this to Eros. He warns her over and over that she is in great danger. He tells her that if she pays attention to her inquiring sisters, there will be a disaster, and he tells her what the disaster will be. If Psyche continues unquestioning, her child (which is now on the way) will be a god, but if she breaks her vow of not questioning, the child will be born a mortal and a girl. And he, Eros, will go away.

Psyche listens and again agrees not to ask questions. But the sisters come and call again. Finally Psyche draws from Eros permission to let them come and visit her. Soon after, the sisters are wafted down from the high crag by the West Wind, and deposited safely in the lovely garden. They admire everything, they are fed and shown about, and of course are green with envy and jealousy at what has happened to their sister. They ask many questions. Poor Psyche, not up to this interrogation, says that her husband is a very young man with the first down of beard on his face, and that he spends his time hunting. She heaps extravagant presents upon her sisters and sends them home.

Eros warns again, and yet again, but the sisters come back. This time Psyche, forgetting what she has told them before, says her husband is a middle-aged man with greying hair and a strong man in the affairs of the world. After the sisters leave, they discuss this and hatch up a venomous plan between them. When they come a third time they tell Psyche that her husband is actually a serpent, a loathsome creature, and when the baby is born, he plans to devour both mother and child!

The sisters have a plan to avert this. They advise Psyche to get a lamp, put it in a covered vessel, and have it ready in the bedchamber. They also tell her to take the sharpest knife available and have it beside her on the couch. In the middle of the night, when her husband is fast asleep, she must sever the head of this loathsome creature with her knife.

Psyche is taken in by all this, and makes these preparations, a light that can be un-covered in the middle of the night, and a knife which she whets to fine sharpness.

Eros comes to the couch after dark and falls asleep beside Psyche. In the night she takes the cover off the lamp, grasps the knife, stands over her husband, and looks at him. To her utter amazement, bewilderment, and guilt, she sees that he is a god, the god of love, and the most beautiful creature in all of Mt. Olympus. She is so shaken and terri-fied by this that she thinks of killing herself. She fumbles with the knife and drops it. She pricks herself accidentally on one of Eros' arrows and, of course, falls in love with him.

She jostles the lamp and a drop of oil from it falls on Eros' right shoulder, and he wakes in pain from the hot oil. He sees what has happened and, being a winged creature, takes flight. Poor Psyche clings to him and is carried a little way with him, out of Paradise.

But she soon falls to the earth in exhaustion and desolation. Eros lights nearby. He says that she has disobeyed; she has broken her covenant. He tells her that, as he had warned her, her child will be born a mortal and that he, Eros, will go away and punish her by his absence. Then he flies away.

This is a drama reproduced and replayed in marriage after marriage countless times. What does this archaic, poetic, mythic language tell us about woman and her relationship to man?

The sisters are those nagging voices within, and often without. Once I was tuning a harpsichord of a friend and couldn't help overhearing the conversation of a coffee klatch going on in the kitchen. Several women were egging each other on to criticize their husbands and their marriages. Here were the two sisters. It affected me so much that I quietly packed up and left. I could not stay in the presence of that venomous talk. Here were the sisters at work.

There is, of course, the positive side, too. The sisters cause Psyche to become conscious, to know Eros as he is, but this consciousness is won at such high cost! It meant overturning the old order. And this is often so. For consciousness, we are apt to pay a Promethean cost.

I am personally terrified of the sister quality in a woman, but it is useful and essential in its place. It does not necessarily follow that one becomes conscious because the nagging sisters appear. One can get stuck there and go no further. One can get stuck at any point. There are women, for example, who are chained on the mountain of death all the rest of their lives. Their relationship with men is then colored by their picture of man as a frightening emissary of death.

Some women do experience love as the devouring dragon, and in that case the sisters are telling the truth. Neumann says that Psyche was devoured by death. Eros comes, and beautiful as he is, he *is* death to her. All husbands are death to their wives in that they destroy them as maidens and force them into an evolution toward mature womanhood. It is paradoxical, but one is both grateful and resentful to the person who sets one on the path of evolution. The oracle was right. A man is death to a woman in an archetypal sense. When a man sees an anguished look on his wife's face, this is a time to be gentle and cautious; it may be that she is just waking up to the fact that she is dying a little as maiden. He can make it easier for her at this moment if he understands.

Usually a man doesn't understand this death-resurrection in a woman as he has no parallel of it in his own life. Marriage is not a sacrificial matter to a man, but that is its chief characteristic for a woman. She looks at her husband in horror one day because she realizes she is caught, trapped, at his mercy. If she has children for a man, she is so much more under his subjection; she is tied to him.

The truth is, a woman goes through a bewildering series of relationships with her husband. He is the god of love, and he is death on the top of the mountain; he is the unknown one in paradise, and he is the censoring one when she demands consciousness. And finally he is the god of love at the summit of Olympus when and if she comes to her own goddesshood. All this is simply bewildering to a man. Small wonder if many a man peers around the door a little gingerly when he comes home each day to see which role is waiting for him. Add to this his own anima involvements and it makes a complex story, but a beautiful one.

The sisters are the demand for evolution from an unexpected source. They may be Psyche's shadow. Dr. Jung described the shadow elements in a personality as those repressed or unlived sides of a person's total potentiality. Through lack of attention and development, these unlived and repressed qualities remain archaic, or turn dark and threatening. These potentialities for good and evil, though repressed, remain in the unconscious, where they gather energy until finally they begin to erupt arbitrarily into our conscious lives, just as the sisters came into Psyche's life.

If we see ourselves consciously as pure loveliness and gentleness only, as Psyche apparently did, we are overlooking this dark side and it may emerge to push us out of our self-satisfied, naive paradise into new discoveries about our true depths.

Dr. Jung said that the demand for evolution in consciousness often comes from the shadow. So the sisters, those less lovely, less perfect representatives of the more ordinary, down-to-earth femininity, may be shadow elements in the Psyche myth.*

* C. S. Lewis treats this aspect of the myth—Psyche's naive identification with her own loveliness and the less lovely sisters' reaction to it—in his book, *Till We Have Faces.*, William B. Eerdmans Publishing Company, 1956.

5

Eros has worked as hard as he can to keep Psyche unconscious. He promised her paradise if she would not look at him. In this way he sought to dominate her.

A woman usually lives some time during her life under the domination of the man within her, or the god within her, the animus. Her own inner Eros keeps her, and quite without her conscious awareness, in paradise. She may not question; she may not have a real relationship with him; she is completely subject to his hidden domination.

It is one of the great dramas in the

interior life of a woman when she challenges the animus' supremacy and says, "I *will* look at you." And when she looks, she sees something beyond the human—a god, or an archetype—but in so doing she plunges herself into a loneliness that is nearly unendurable. That is why the stalemate, the domination, the time in paradise, goes on for so long. A woman knows intuitively that if she breaks up this state of animus possession, it brings the most hellish kind of loneliness.

Many women experience but do not recognize the animus' autonomy over them. I remember a woman who came to see me and related a dream in which she had made something that was precious to her. The animus figure in the dream said, "Give it to me." And she did. I rose straight up in the air when I heard this. I said to her, "You go back and re-do that dream, and you tell him that he may not have it."

However, once a woman *sees* the animus, he can no longer be dominant in her psyche. When she knows she has an animus and she relates to him, she is no longer subservient.

The child promised to Psyche by Eros will be a god (totally unconscious) if she obeys and does as she is told—asks no questions, and does not light the lamp of consciousness to see her Eros nature as it truly is. This is a possibility, and it may be that a woman will want to live in this timeless primordial way, but she will be alien to the modern world if she does. Almost all modern women ask the questions, light the lamp, and insist on their own consciousness.

One of the most rewarding bits of symbolism in our story is the instruction given by the two sisters. Psyche is advised to provide herself with a light and a knife, two masculine symbols. It is exceedingly useful if a woman can understand her capacity to wield these two instruments. What does a wife do that is lamp-like and what does she do that is knife-like? The sisters even tell Psyche what joint to cut through, the joint between the head and the rest of the body, to behead this terrible monster.

I think we can state it as a profound and powerful law: a woman should use the lamp, but not the knife. The knife is for private use, for discrimination, for clarity, for cutting through the fogbanks. It is for internal use. If a woman could remember to use the lamp first in the difficult times in her marriage, then she could choose whether or not to use the knife, or where to use it. Usually the knife comes out first. Then she gets out the lamp to see what she has done.

The knife is that devastating capacity a woman has of impaling a man with a flow of words: it is the devastating remark that skewers a man. This is also one of the ways a man's anima, his feminine side, behaves when he is in poor relationship to it. It is cutting and sarcastic; it comes with knife in hand. Our law, to use the lamp and not the knife, applies equally to the man's inner anima as well as to the outer woman.

35

What then, is the lamp, and what does it show? It revealed that Eros was a god. A woman has the capacity to show the value of her man with the lamp of her consciousness. At his best, a man knows who he is, and he knows he has a god, a magnificent being, somewhere within him. But when a woman lights the lamp and sees the god in him, he feels called upon to live up to that, to be strong in his consciousness. Naturally he trembles! Yet he seems to require this feminine acknowledgment of his worth. Terrible things happen to men who are deprived of the presence of women, for apparently it is the presence of women that reminds each man of the best that is in him.

During World War II, there were isolated groups of men stationed in the Aleutians. They could not be relieved properly because of transportation problems. None of the entertainment groups went near them. More than half of these men suffered nervous breakdowns. They wouldn't shave; they wouldn't cut their hair; morale broke down entirely. Perhaps it was because there was no woman, no Psyche looking upon Eros, to remind the men of their worth.

If a man is a bit discouraged, a woman can just look at him and restore him to his sense of value. There seems to be a peculiar vacant spot in a man's psychology here. Most men get their deepest conviction of self worth from a woman, their wife or mother, or, if they are highly conscious, from their own anima. The woman sees and shows the man his value by lighting the lamp.

I was sitting in on a family quarrel once when a woman was wielding a knife vigorously. Far down on the list of her husband's transgressions was the complaint that he got home from the office so late. He said, "Don't you understand that I stay at the office for you?" The woman collapsed. She had heard something, for once. Never before had she stopped talking long enough to hear. He said, "I wouldn't go to the office except for you. I don't like the office. I work for you." There was a sudden new dimension in that marriage. The woman could have seen this if she had lit the lamp and looked.

A man depends largely on the woman for the light in the family as he is not very good at finding meaning for himself. Life is often dry and barren for him unless someone bestows meaning on life for him. With a few words, a woman can give meaning to a whole day's struggle, and a man will be very grateful. A man knows and wants this; he will edge up to it; he will initiate little occasions so that a woman can shed some light for him. When he comes home and recounts the events of the day, he is asking her to bestow meaning on them. This is part of the light-bearing quality of a woman.

The touch of light, or acknowledgment, is a fiery thing. It often stings a man into awareness, which is partly why he fears the feminine so much. A woman, or his anima, often leads a man into new consciousness. It is almost always the woman who says, "Let's sit down and talk about where we are." A man does not often say this. The woman is the carrier of evolution for him in one way or another. She sometimes lights him into a new kind of relationship. The man is terrified of that, but he is equally terrified at the loss of it. Actually, a man greatly appreciates a woman who bears a lamp; he depends on the feminine light more deeply than most men are willing to admit.

The oil is a feminine quality. I remember someone's speaking of the old lamps that used vegetable oil and moss wicks. The oil of olive is very feminine. And we also have the phrase, "to be boiled in oil!" A symbol always has two sides to it. The oil supplies the light, but it also burns Eros.

Feminine light is exquisitely beautiful. There is nothing finer than the light which a woman gives forth. It is the Jewish custom for the woman to light the sabbath candles on Friday evenings. One would think it would be the man, but it is the woman. It is she who begins the sabbath; she who provides the light.

The symbolism of the lamp in the myth points to the light-bearing capacity of women. In the Eleusinian mysteries, the women often carry torches, which shed a peculiarly feminine kind of light. A torch softly lights up the immediate surroundings, shows the practical next step to be taken. This is unlike the cosmic masculine light of the sun that lights up so much territory one is sometimes overwhelmed and lost to the immediate experience.

On the other hand, women have the knife that can wound or kill. The man is vulnerable to both of these.

Very few women understand how great is the hunger in a man to be near femininity. This should not be a burden for a woman. She doesn't have to live her whole life feminizing. For as a man discovers and gets into good relationship with his own inner femininity, he will not rely so heavily on the outer woman to live this out for him. But if a woman wishes to give a most precious gift to a man, if she would truly feed this greatest masculine hunger (a hunger which he will seldon show but which is always there), she will be very, very feminine when her man is in a mood, so he can get his bearings and be a man again.

6

Now comes the thorniest, but most rewarding part of the myth. First Eros pricked his finger on his own love arrows and was catapulted into falling in love with Psyche. In a way, that is what upset, or set up, the whole thing. Eros was sent to get Psyche to fall in love with a monster, with Death itself, that most hideous of beasts, but he pricked his finger on one of his own arrows and fell in love with Psyche. Then she brought forth the lamp to look at her supposedly demon husband, and saw that he was the god of love. Then she accidentally pricked her finger on one of his arrows and fell in love with the god of love. This is a most puzzling thing. Psyche fell in love with love.

The quality of "being in love" is a super-human quality that mankind is not yet able to bear easily. When it happens to one, one is wafted off to realms that intoxicate, to super-ordinate levels of consciousness that, almost without exception, are beyond one's capacity to live.

We must differentiate *loving* and *being in love.* To try to make definitions of these takes some courage.

Loving another person is seeing that person truly, and appreciating him for what he actually is, his ordinariness, his failures, and his magnificence. If one can ever cut through that fog of projections in which one lives so much of his life, and can look truly at another person, that person, in his down to earth individuality is a magnificent creature. The trouble is that there are so many people, and we are so blinded by our own projections, we rarely see another clearly in all his depth and nobility.

Once I tried an experiment, imagining that all of the people on earth were gone except one other person and myself. I went out on the sidewalks to see if I could find that one remaining person, to see what that person would be like and how I would welcome him. I found someone. For a little while I saw the miracle of what another human being can be. There was just one, and that one became infinitely valuable. A true marvel.

Loving is something like that. It is seeing another person for the down-to-earth, practical, immediate experience which another human being is. Loving is not illusory. It is not seeing the other person in a particular role or image we have designed for him. Loving is valuing another for his personal uniqueness within the context of the ordinary world. That is durable. It stands up. It is real. If someone had told me ten or fifteen years ago that I would be equating love and durability, I would have been shocked and angry, but I suppose this is a wisdom that middle age brings.

Being *in love* is another matter. Being in love is an intrusion, for better or for worse, of an archetypal, a superpersonal or divine world. Suddenly one sees in one's beloved a god or a goddess, through him or her one sees into a superpersonal, superconscious realm of being. All this is highly explosive and inflammatory, a divine madness. The poets tell us about it in extravagant terms.

If one watches people in love looking at each other, one knows perfectly well that they are looking *through* each other. Each is in love with an idea, or an ideal, or an emotion. They are in love with love. The women are Psyche, seeing Eros in his role as the god of love, rather than as a person whom she knows and loves for himself.

The worst thing about being in love is that it is not durable; it doesn't last. One day the bright vision of the beloved, which had previously danced with such beauty before one's eyes, seems plain and dull. The transpersonal godlike quality dims, and the personal, down-to-earth, ordinary man is revealed. This is one of the saddest and most painful experiences in life. The quality of being in love is a visitation of something divine. It is a god or a goddess on the face of the earth, and does not fit at all well into human dimensions.

So what is the myth saying? The god of love himself, Eros, is pricked by one of his own arrows and falls in love with a mortal. Apparently the gods can get by with this. It is not too difficult for the god of love to be assailed by the experience of being in love because it is his nature.

Yet even the Olympians are afraid of Eros; those arrows send even the highest of the gods and goddesses into a panic. Even they are vulnerable; and the god of love himself knows the experience of being in love.

But when a mere mortal suddenly is pricked by that fatal arrow and falls in love, it is very serious. It was said that Psyche's rash look at Eros was the first time in history that a mortal has ever encountered a god or goddess and survived. Prior to this, when a mortal came into contact with a god or goddess, he was incinerated, obliterated by the power of the encounter.

Translated into psychological terms, one can say that prior to this point in the evolution of mankind, if a man or woman actually touched an archetype, he/she was simply obliterated. The myth is telling us that henceforth, and under certain circumstances, when a mere mortal undergoes an archetypal experience, he may survive it, but will be radically changed by it. I think this is what our story is teaching us. A mortal is touching something of supermortal dimensions and lives to tell the tale. Within this context, one can see what it means to be touched by the arrows of the god of being-in-love. One can see the enormity of it, the transposition of levels involved. This is the incredible, explosive experience of falling in love.

The oriental people do not fall in love. They go at their relationships quietly, undramatically, untouched by the arrows of Eros. Marriages are arranged. Traditionally the man doesn't see his bride until the ceremony is over and the veils are lifted from her. Then he takes her home and follows the prescribed pattern for the newly married groom with his bride.

My own western sentiments were touched the other day when I received a letter from a twenty year old Indian whom I don't know well, but with whom I had set up a correspondence. He had worked it out that I would be the perfect husband for his eighteen year old sister, and he wanted to know if I would agree to this. A dowry and such things could be discussed. I went around on a cloud all day. With no effort whatsoever, without even falling in love, I could have a bride, and an eighteen year old one at that. It did my morale no end of good. Then I wrote back and told him that it was not possible, that I was much too old for his sister.

Our story is about a woman who was

touched by something far greater than ordinary human experience. The rest of the myth tells us how to survive this divine touching.

7

At one time the experience of being touched by the gods took place in a religious context, but we moderns have relegated religion to a relatively side issue in our lives. We take it lightly and leave it for Sunday, if we observe it at all. One rarely hears of a person's being profoundly touched by a religious experience. Religion has cooled in our western culture, and we think we are too wise for it. Even the people who cling to traditional religious forms are often not greatly moved by them; they are not nourished in a profound, earth-shaking way in their spiritual, inner life.

It is my contention that this profound encounter, being touched by the splendor or the power of a god, has fallen to our peculiar western notion of falling in love. *There* we are touched.

The myth says that Psyche lights the lamp and sees that she is indeed married to a god. She pricks her finger on one of his arrows and falls in love with love. And almost immediately after, she loses him. How often this is the experience of persons when they see the godhood of another, when they fall in love.

To love is to draw close to another person, to have ties, to merge with the other person. *To be in love* with a person is to look right through him, and thus to lose that person irrevocably. This is bad news. We do not like it, and seldom comprehend what it means.

If one looks at the godhood of another person, one looks at the magnificent, trans-personal dimensions he incorporates. By definition that puts him outside the scope of one's own ordinary realm, unless one has discovered one's own godhood, which is rare. This is why being in love hurts so much. There seems to be a built-in paradox that the moment one falls in love with someone, he must acknowledge that person's utter uniqueness and thus their separateness. In such a situation we are painfully aware of the distance, the separation, and the impossibility of relationship. Also, there is the terrible feeling of inferiority a woman feels when she lights the lamp and discovers that her mate is a god whom she had presumed was a mere mortal. It is a devastating, lonely feeling.

Yet the very act of being torn to bits by being in love presents its own possibility of solution. If one has the strength and courage for it, out of this dismemberment may come a new consciousness of one's own uniqueness and worth. That is a very difficult way to go, but perhaps there is no other way for some temperaments.

The best way to solve this dilemma is to stand absolutely still, and that is what Psyche finally does. Once she gets over her suicidal feelings, she sits still. If one has been dazzled out of one's wits, if one has been knocked totally out of one's orbit, it is best to keep still. One can't tell youth this; it is just not possible. This is wisdom not often heard until our more mature years.

I once had to mediate in a very awkward situation in which two people had fallen in love with one another and were creating considerable wreckage in the close community in which they lived. My advice was to leave them alone, to put no prohibitions on them, and they would balance it themselves. And they did. This is built into the being in love situation. It must have its barriers and its tragedy. Tragedy means seeing a vision one cannot attain. Philosophers and poets tell us that being in love is a tragic situation. I am not talking about *love.* As mentioned before, *loving* someone is warm; it is drawing close, and it is workable. But *being in love,* seeing the godhood of another person, is not humanly workable.

One can translate being-in-love into love. This is what a successful marriage does. A marriage begins in-love and, hopefully, makes the transition to loving. And that, in a way, is what our story is all about. It begins as the story of a collision between a mortal and a god, between two levels of being, between humanness and a superhuman quality. We long for that superhuman quality, and then wonder that we cannot keep it. It is not humanly possible to maintain the quality of in-loveness. I remember a James Thurber cartoon in which a middle-aged couple is quarreling and he hurls back at her, "Well who took the magic out of our marriage!"

When one has been touched by a god or a goddess, what is one to do? That question is largely unanswered in our culture. Most people suffer and endure the fading of the godlike vision of the beloved, settle down into the humdrum of middle age, and think that their vision of a superhuman quality was all a bit foolish anyway. The feminine alternative to this self-defeating and depressing end to being-in-love occupies us for the rest of our story.

Psyche falls back upon her elemental femininity. She seeks out Aphrodite and is given tasks to perform which are stages of evolution in her inner development, at the end of which she is summoned to Olympus and is herself made a goddess. She is married to Eros and gives birth to her child. This is the noblest possible answer to the most perplexing question facing our society.

To be touched by a godlike experience is to become open to learning a godlike consciousness, godlike in a Greek, Olympian sense. The Greeks spoke of the archetypes as gods, a far more poetic and adequate terminology than our modern terms. It is both beautiful and intelligent to speak of god and goddess, Eros and Psyche, who are the great archetypes functioning within us when we have fallen in love. Once this quality has touched us, we can never return to simple, carefree, unconscious ways. Almost always, for a modern person, this touch comes to us when we fall in love with another person. History tells us of many ways men have been touched by that which is greater than themselves, but for *our* time Eros is a principle intermediary between us and the power of God.

8

To move further into the myth, we recall that, when Psyche wounds him, Eros flies home to Aphrodite and does not appear again till the end of the myth. He goes home to mother. This is precisely what almost every man does when his wife wounds him into consciousness; he takes refuge in his mother complex. He may not go home physically, but he retreats into his mother complex and disappears for a while. If a man suddenly becomes silent, is perfunctory and not available, he may have "gone home to mother," and Aphrodite reigns.

On the other hand, if we view Eros as the woman's animus, we may perhaps say that Eros held Psyche in a state of unconscious animus possession in paradise until she lighted the lamp of consciousness and then, as animus, he flew back into the inner world.

Dr. Jung said that the anima and animus function most effectively for us as mediators between the conscious and unconscious parts of the personality. When Eros returns to the inner world of Aphrodite, he is able to mediate for Psyche with Aphrodite, Zeus and the other gods and goddesses of the inner archetypal world. As we shall see, he is able to send Psyche help at critical times in her development by using natural, earthly elements such as the ants, the eagle and the reeds.

One might say that for a woman to evolve, she must break the unconscious domination of her subordinate, largely unconscious masculine component which dictates, often negatively, her relationship to the outer world. For her to evolve, the animus, consciously recognized as such, must take up a position between the conscious ego and the unconscious inner world where he can act as mediator, an essential help to her.

A woman in a state of animus possession is not consciously aware of her animus at all. She assumes that behavior arising from the animus is her own ego-originated behavior. In actual fact, her ego is taken over in these instances by the animus. However, when a woman lights the lamp of consciousness, she sees the animus, quite correctly, as separate from her ego. Like Psyche, she is usually overwhelmed. The animus seems so potent and godlike, and her conscious ego self so worthless and helpless by comparison. This is a desperate and dangerous moment for a woman. But it is not the end. After she goes through the awesome shock of first truly recognizing her animus and being overwhelmed with her own seeming inadequacy in comparison, she is then equally overwhelmed by his grandeur. If one sees that one has a godlike element within, the result is an exhilirating reaction, a peak experience, much like what happens when one falls in love.

When Psyche lighted the lamp, she expected to see a beast, but she saw a god. To women, man is often either a god or a beast. When I have the courage, I can say that when one truly shows the light upon another person, he finds a god or a goddess. I do not know any greater affirmation that one can have than to be told that when one truly looks at his or her mate, one finds a god or goddess. The same is true when a woman is finally able consciously to see her animus, her inner Eros. She finds that he is godlike.

This event for Psyche is in some ways comparable to Parsifal's first sight of the grail castle. Parsifal sees a magnificent world beyond belief, but he is not to remain there. Likewise, Psyche loses Eros almost immediately upon discovering his true and magnificent nature as a god.

In her devastation at having seen Eros

fly away, Psyche immediately wants to drown herself in a river. At each difficult point, Psyche wants to kill herself. Does this not point toward a kind of self-sacrifice— sacrificing one level of consciousness for another? Most people are repelled by this, but it is essential. If we can get back to its archetypal meaning, we can profit by it. When a woman is touched by an archetypal experience, she will collapse before it. A man loses contact with his grail castle and is sometimes many long years recovering it. But a woman does not leave her grail castle, at least not for long, and it is in her collapse that she quickly recovers her archetypal connection. This may not be a happy moment for a woman, but it restores inner connections and makes a positive and helpful quality available for her assistance.

It is bewildering to a man to discover the degree to which a woman has control over her feelings, a capacity unknown to most men. A woman can enter the grail castle almost at will; she can go to a feminine touchstone when she chooses to. And that is most beautiful! An analogous performance is much more difficult for a man to do. A woman still must go through her tasks, but she has the help of that highly introverted, inturned quality which is Psyche-type femininity's way of responding to the god touch she experiences.

Psyche sits and waits for a solution. A man has to pocket his knife (sword, weapon), mount his new horse (bike, car) and go out and accomplish something. The feminine way, by woman or by anima, is to wait until something in her gives her the means and the way and the courage.

We are not so much talking about male and female here, as about masculine and feminine. The feminine way of giving up is similar, if not the same, as that of the Rainmaker in Tao. A man can do this by acting out of his feminine side. It is a divine giving up.

A woman, or the feminine principle, seems to have to go back to a very still inner center every time something happens to her; and this is a creative act. She must go back to it, but must not drown in it. She is receptive, not passive.

I remember a very wise woman I once knew who, when I would pour out all of my woes, would say, "Wait." That was terrible for me. My horse was already pawing with impatience. I did not want to be told to wait, but it was right to do so; right, that is, if the problem happened to be a feminine one.

During World War II, when I worked for the American Red Cross, I went in to my supervisor's office and poured out all my excitement, saying, "This has happened, and this has happened, and this has happened, and what shall I do?" She looked at me, and said quietly, "You go to lunch." She knew.

It is that feminine quality of getting back to stillness that is the sacrifice. It is observed in the Christian tradition when we say, "Here we offer and present unto Thee ourselves, ... a living sacrifice."

Psyche makes the sacrifice. She goes to

the river to give herself up, perhaps with the wrong motives, but with the right instincts.

Pan, the cloven-footed god with Echo in his lap, is sitting by the river. He sees that Psyche is about to drown herself, and dissuades her. I have always read that, have smiled, and have gone on, but one has no right to go past anything in a myth. Why is it that Pan is the one who saves Psyche from the wrong kind of stillness?

We get the word panic from the god Pan. It is that feeling of being beside oneself, that wild quality, that near madness the ancients thought so highly of and we regret so bitterly when we get into it. This is the factor that helps Psyche. This myth is full of tiny observations or advice to one about what to do when one is stuck or overwhelmed. The advice at the moment is to go to Pan, the cloven-footed god. It is this god, so strange to our modern mentality, who can connect us again with earth and instinct in the right way, not in a suicidal way.

A woman's fit of weeping is a Pan reaction. Sometimes in a crisis it is a necessary and good reaction for her to have. If her husband is one who cannot stand to see a woman cry, she may simply have to put him through it anyway. Pan has something to say to her, and perhaps to him, in moments like these.

Pan tells Psyche that she must pray to the god of love, who understands when someone is inflamed by love. Here is a nice irony, that one must go to the very god who has wounded one to ask for one's relief. But it is good advice.

Being the god of love, Eros is the god of relationship. I think we can say that when a woman is in difficulty, she must turn to, must be loyal to Eros, to relationship. She must take it as her guiding principle, go the way consistent with relationship.

Psyche prays, she goes to the altars of the many goddesses instead of to Eros to ask for help, and she is rejected time after time. Each of the goddesses fears Aphrodite and will not anger her by helping Psyche.

At this stage in the grail myth, Parsifal is red-knighting, fighting heroic battles with all his energy. Psyche is going from altar to altar, praying. This is the same work as the man's—equal work, noble work, but differently done.

Psyche must continue to suffer until her way is clear. Fritz Kunkel once said that no one has the right to pull someone out of suffering prematurely. Psyche must go her way. If one is on the path of suffering, or in one of these dry patches, sometimes one must just stay dry for a time. But if one understands the overall structure of one's suffering, a local dry patch is not so devastating or frightening.

Many of the women of the Bible had to suffer. Christ on the cross is suffering in His way, and the women at the foot of the cross are suffering in theirs.

Finally Psyche realizes that she must go to Aphrodite herself, because it is she who holds the key to all of her difficulties. And she does.

A bitter, tyrannical speech is given by Aphrodite. Psyche is reduced to nothing. She is told that she is good for nothing except to be a scullery maid, and that if there is any place in the world for her, which is doubtful, it is to be set to the lowest tasks possible. Which is precisely what Aphrodite proceeds to do. The first of the four famous tasks is laid out for Psyche, as a condition for her deliverance.

9

Aphrodite shows Psyche a huge pile of seeds of many different kinds, mixed together, and tells her she must sort these seeds before nightfall or the penalty will be death. Then Aphrodite sweeps off in grandeur to a wedding festival. Poor Psyche is left with this impossible task which no one could conceivably do. So she sits still again, and waits.

We may assume that Eros, as animus, now back in the inner world and no longer with Psyche in a state of unconscious animus possession, is able to mediate for her and to aid her in finding the strength and wisdom she needs to accomplish her tasks.

We assume that it is through him that the ants hear of Psyche's dilemma and sort the seeds for her. By dusk the task is completed, and when Aphrodite comes back to check on the situation, she grudgingly allows that for a no-good like Psyche this is adequate.

What a beautiful bit of symbolism; a pile of seeds to sort! In many of the practical matters of life, in the running of a household, for example, a woman's task is to see that form, or order, prevails. That is sorting. What household has not echoed to the cry of, "Mom, where is my other sock?"

A man goes to a woman for this household sorting. The man is off to more important things, as he sees it, in the affairs of the world, and it is left to the woman to keep order in his home life. Yet a man typically does not think of a woman as being well able to sort, to discriminate, to order.

When a man makes love to a woman, he gives her seeds past comprehension, millions of seeds. She has to choose one. There, on a very rudimentary level, is the sorting. It is she who chooses, unconsciously in this case, which of these many, many seeds to develop. Nature in its excess produces so much, and the woman sorts.

In other departments of life, a woman is flooded with things to sort. When the household quiets down, a woman is left with a bewildering array of possibilities. This is hard on pure feminine nature, which has been described by Irene de Castellejo as diffused awareness, as opposed to masculine nature which is focused consciousness.

Most cultures try to solve this through custom and law by stipulating what a woman shall do to save her from having to sort. But we are a free people and we have no such safeguards, so a woman must know how to differentiate, how to sort creatively. To do this she needs to find her ant nature, that primitive, chthonic, earthy quality which will help her. The ant nature is not of the intellect; it does not give us rules to follow; it is a primitive, instinctive, quiet quality; perhaps a masculine attribute, yet legitimately available to women.

It is profitable for a woman to gain some proficiency in this seed sorting attribute. One might do one's tasks in a kind of geometric way, the nearest one first, or the one closest to one's feeling value first. In this primitive, simple, earthy way one can break the impass of too-muchness.

Perhaps this seed sorting attribute is a part of woman's inner masculinity—an echo of Eros. But a woman must remember *this* basic law, that she use this cool, dry, highly discriminating function which is her animus as a connection between her conscious ego and the inner world, the collective unconscious. The animus (and anima) belong primarily in the heavens and the hells of the inner world. Animus and anima are curiously part human and part god, part personal and part transpersonal. That is why they make such excellent intermediaries between the personality and the collective unconscious. They have a foot in each world: they function best as inner spiritual guides for the conscious ego as it goes about the world.

We often depreciate the animus, but that is justified only when it is used in the wrong place. If it appears outwardly, it usually makes trouble, but it *is* a key to one's spiritual life when it functions inwardly. It is the chief connection between us as individuals and that great inner oneness, the godhead, the collective unconscious. That is where the animus truly belongs.

I think we are in trouble in our basic attitude toward sorting these days. The modern woman rebels against this act of sorting for her family, for instance, but it is a primary requirement for her development. I hasten to say that she should not have to sort things that do not belong to her. To have to sort too many objective things in the outside world is not required of all women. An amazon type (as defined in Tony Wolff's description of the four types of woman as mother, hetaira, medium and amazon), or a business woman can cope with such sorting. She has a highly developed ant nature, and can use her masculine component in the outer world.

Another kind of feminine sorting is not so well known these days. I think we trip over it and come to grief with it. The feminine in a woman, or the anima in a man, must sort out the influx of material from the unconscious and relate it properly and orderly to consciousness. This is, in my mind, the great feminine function, often overlooked in our culture.

The masculine component in personality, in man and woman, deals primarily with the outer world, while the feminine component deals primarily with the inner world.

A fine image of a marriage partnership is one in which the man and woman stand back to back, he facing the outer world where he is more at home, and she the inner world where she is more at home. But this is not a static situation; they each, hopefully, move toward wholeness, which is the total Janus-faced personality facing at once the inner and the outer worlds.

Ideally one might imagine the man and woman as two circles overlapping. In the beginning of their psychological development there is very little overlapping; the man deals with and protects the family from the outer world, while the woman deals with and protects the family from the inner world. Gradually, as the woman and the man each develop sufficiently their own capacities to face in both directions, the circles move together and the overlap is deeper.

It often happens today that both partners face toward the outer world and neither is aware of the unconscious or inner world. The family is left unguarded at this point. I would urge women to take up their natural and noble work of facing and mediating the inner world for themselves, for their husbands and families, and for society, while helping others to learn to see the inner world for themselves. Sorting out the influx of emotions, moods, and archetypes for the family is a beautiful feminine act.

10

The second of Psyche's tasks, arrogantly and insultingly set out by Aphrodite, is to go to a certain field across a river and get some of the golden fleece of the rams which are pastured there. She is to be back by nightfall, on pain of death.

Psyche must be very brave (foolhardy is a better word—for the rams are very fierce) if she is to accomplish this dangerous task. Once more she collapses and thinks of suicide. She goes toward the river which separates her from the field of the sun rams intending to throw herself in. But just at the critical moment the reeds in the river's edge speak to her and give her advice.

The reeds tell Psyche not to go near the rams during the daylight hours to get the wool—she would immediately be battered to death—but to go at dusk and take some of their wool which has been brushed off by the brambles and low hanging boughs of a grove of trees which stand in the field, and under which the rams often pass. There she will get enough of the golden fleece to satisfy Aphrodite without even attracting the attention of the rams. Psyche is told not to go directly to the rams or try to take the golden fleece by force because they are dangerous beasts with an aggressive, bullheaded quality, and can kill her. Some masculinity looks like this to women. Every woman needs to learn to relate with courage to the outer world, a natural masculine trait, but she knows instinctively that too much is fatal, and even to go near is dangerous. Imagine a very feminine woman at the beginning of her life looking at the modern world and knowing that she must make her way through it. She fears that she will be killed! Just walking downtown and coming home again is frightening. One can be bludgeoned to death, depersonalized by the ram nature of the patriarchal, competitive, impersonal society in which we live.

A distinction needs to be made here between rams and fleece. Perhaps we should go back briefly to the myth of the quest for the golden fleece to gain some insight about Psyche's task.

The quest for the golden fleece is one of the great masculine myths of antiquity. In it

Jason and his friends prove their courage, strength and virility. Edith Hamilton says of the quest, "each of the finest men in Greece who came with Jason has a desire not to be left behind nursing a life without peril by his mother's side, but even at the price of death to drink with his comrades the peerless elixir of valor."

The famous golden fleece was the fleece of a ram who saved two youths, the girl Helle and the boy Phrixos, from death at the hands of their father and stepmother. A mighty ram flew in at the last moment, gathered the prince and princess up and flew away with them. Unfortunately, the girl was dropped into the sea and drowned. The boy, when he was safely set down in another kingdom, killed the ram as a sacrifice of thanksgiving. The golden fleece was then given to the king of that land by Phrixos. It was much later that Jason and the others came in search of it from Phrixos' homeland.

We can see that the ram represents a mighty power capable of saving a person from a parental situation that threatens his life. It represents a great, elemental, natural force which one can tap at times through an archetype, or it can erupt unexpectedly as an invading complex within a personality. This power is awesome and numinous. It is the burning bush, it is the vast unconscious depths that can sweep aside the frail ego if it is not in the right connection to it.

A man may have access to or be taken over by the ram force at times, but he should not identify with it. It is no accident that in the myth the girl dropped back into the sea and drowned. A man in the throes of a ram complex is not in relationship with his inner femininity—it is lost in the unconscious, in the sea. In the grail myth we learned that women did not fare well while the men were red-knighting. Ramming seems in some ways similar to red-knighting. In either case, femininity suffers.

As mentioned above, after Phrixos was safely set down again on earth, he piously sacrificed the ram, retaining the golden fleece, which is the logos symbol. There is as close and organic a connection between logos and power as there is between fleece and ram. Modern western man, using his logos, his rational scientific mind, has found a way to tap the sources of power in his universe. By so doing, he has accrued awesome power over other men and over nature. Modern technological man has assumed a godlike quantity of power, and is in danger of destroying his world with it.

How shall he manage this awesome power to his own and nature's advantage? The ancient myths tell us: sacrifice the ram and keep the fleece, or take only that fleece which has pulled off on the bushes and cannot cause an eruption of ram madness. Or, as the modern myth maker Tolkien tells us, throw the ring of power back into the earth. Or, in eastern terminology, keep a balance between Yang and Yin, between logos and Eros. The Psyche myth says one must not try to take or use the fleece that still grows on the rams; elemental knowledge connected to elemental power is capable of destroying instantaneously.

Modern man needs to give up his god-like assumption of unnatural power over nature and the destiny of the entire world. His logos has led him into a fixation with power, into an inflated identification with the ram, and he is not an adequate carrier of that force. Just as a person who gets too close to an archetype is obliterated, a person identifying with the ram will also be destroyed.

John Sanford observes that if a young person takes drugs before he has developed a strong enough ego to withstand the massive interior experience he may encounter, he may be obliterated. We moderns, men and women, are grasping a ram of massive proportions which may turn on us and destroy us. Should we not give up naked power plays and keep logos in proper proportion with Eros and relatedness, relatedness to each other and to nature?

Perhaps the myth's statement of *how* much fleece and *how* much logos, speaks not only to women, but also to men. We can handle only as much logos as will not cause an eruption of power that will destroy us, personally or collectively.

There is a distinction between the masculine and the feminine way of obtaining the fleece; between the way Phrixos acquires it and the way Psyche acquires it. Phrixos must kill the ram sacrificially. Psyche need not kill the ram; she is to avoid direct contact with it and gather fleece from the branches and boughs. The idea of having to take the remnants, just the scrapings of logos off the boughs, may sound intolerable to a modern woman. Why should a woman have to get just a little of this quality? Why can't she simply pin down the ram, take his fleece, and go with it in triumph as a man does?

Delilah accomplished her masculine need in just this way, a power play. The Psyche myth tells us that a woman can get the necessary masculinity for her purposes without a power play. Psyche's way is much gentler. I think this is the place where I part company with the feminist movement. If a woman wants to wield some masculine power, which I agree with, she need not gain it in the masculine way.

There are women who need a greater share of masculinity than the myth indicates. One is reminded of the amazons who took off their left breasts (which meant giving up a significant part of their femininity) so that they could draw a bow without the breast getting in the way of the bowstring when it was released. More masculinity may mean less femininity, and this is just the problem.

It is my feeling that western civilization took a wrong turn some time ago, and the place of femininity is in jeopardy now. That is why this myth is so important. It talks about a right way and a wrong way for a woman to function. It is saying that a woman can get all she really needs of masculinity in a noncompetitive way.

The myth is in no way saying that a woman may not have fleece, or that she may not use her focused consciousness, her masculine component. It is saying that just as a man will only be hampered by an excess of the feminine quality, so a woman requires only a little of the fleece.

Actually, at the time the myth of Psyche emerged, the very idea that Psyche should have *any* of the fleece was novel indeed. Until that time, the quest for the golden fleece was a masculine quest, a great masculine adventure. To obtain a bit of the golden fleece, required Psyche to find and use her own courage, valor, adventuring spirit and strength. This task was necessary for the development of women beyond the purely instinctive unconscious feminine stage. To be sent out to gather fleece was a great advance for womankind.

And we must remember too, that a microcosm is a macrocosm. A bit of the logos is all of the logos. One is reminded of the story of Christ who was walking amidst a great crowd, jostled and touched by many people around him. Yet one woman, in a right attitude, had only to touch the hem of his garment and she was healed and made whole.

The myth tells us that the feminine need only obtain a bit of the fleece, the hem, not the whole garment, to have enough for her purposes, to be made whole.

When we talk of a woman's acquiring fleece, or masculinity, we must understand that we are not striving for an equal amount of masculinity and femininity within ourselves. Many women say they want just as much focused consciousness as a man. This is not reasonable or safe. One must be a woman with masculinity backing her up, or one must be a man with femininity backing him up. The masculinity in a woman is a minority. We all have such limits, dictated by biological limits or functions. The woman who understands this can go into the business world and use her objective masculinity. She brings, along with a focused consciousness, her quietness, her touch with the source, her quality of reminding those around her of the grail castle.

When raising a teenage boy, a woman should know this principle: she should not seek to know too much too quickly, she must not snatch the boy's world from him, take his sword away from him. A boy's masculine world is fragile and vulnerable, especially if confronted suddenly and aggressively by his mother's own masculine side.

11

Back to the myth, Aphrodite now appears and discovers that, incredibly, Psyche *has* the bit of golden fleece. In her anger, she decides to really defeat Psyche. She tells the girl that she must fill a crystal goblet with water from the Styx, a river that tumbles from a high mountain, disappears into the earth, and comes back to the high mountain again. It is a circular stream, ever returning to its source, down into the depths of hell and back up to the highest crag again. This stream is guarded by dangerous monsters, and there is no place where one can set foot near enough to the stream to get even one little goblet of water from it.

True to form, Psyche collapses, but this time she is numb with defeat and cannot even cry. Then an eagle of Zeus appears.

The eagle assisted Zeus in a certain amorous episode earlier, so eagle and Zeus have a certain camaraderie. Zeus, now willing to protect his son Eros openly, asks the eagle to assist Psyche. The eagle flies to her in her distress, and asks her to give him the crystal goblet. Flying to the center of the stream, he lowers the goblet into the dangerous waters and fills it for her, brings the vessel safely back to Psyche, and her task is accomplished.

The river is the river of life; it flows high and low, from the high mountains down into the depths of the earth. The current of the river is fast flowing and treacherous; the banks are slippery and steep. Approaching too closely, one could easily be swept off and drowned in the waters or crushed on the rocks below.

I think that this task is telling us how the feminine must relate to the vastness of life. She may take only one goblet of water. The feminine way is to do one thing and to do it well. She is not denied a second or third or tenth thing, but she must take it one goblet at a time, each in good order.

The feminine aspect of the human psyche has been described by some psychologists as unfocused consciousness. The feminine nature is flooded with the rich vastness of possibilities in life, and is drawn to all of them, usually all at once. The difficulty with this is that it is impossible; one cannot do or be everything at once. Many of the possibilities open to us oppose each other and one must choose among them. Like the eagle, who has a panoramic vision, one must look at the vast river, focus on a single spot, and then dip out a single goblet of water.

There is a heresy abroad today which states that if a little is good, more is better. The advertisements tell us to "grab all the gusto we can" in life. This will not work. It means that one is never satisfied. Even while one is engaged in one rich experience, he is looking about for other possibilities. He is never content with anything because he is always searching for something bigger and better.

Our myth tells us that a little of a quality, experienced in high consciousness, is sufficient for us. As the poet tells us, we may see the world in a grain of sand. We can focus on one aspect of life, or one experience, concentrate on it, drink it in, and be satisfied. Then we can move on to whatever new experience may follow in good order.

The crystal goblet is the container in which the water is to be held. Crystal is, of course, very fragile and very precious. The human ego may be compared to the crystal goblet. It is a container for some of the vastness of the river of life. If the ego container, like the goblet, is not carefully related to the beautiful but treacherous river, it can be shattered. One needs an eagle nature to see clearly to dip into the river at the right places and in the right manner. Perhaps too, the ego that is attempting to raise to consciousness some of the vast unconscious depths within, can be well advised to try to scoop up and contain only one goblet of water at a time lest he be overwhelmed and his ego container shattered.

The earthbound individual who approaches the river of life from the ground, from a point along its banks, from one single spot along its vast reaches, may, on the one hand, look down into a crashing, swirling confusion and feel that there is no way to sort it all out. Or, if he approaches the river from another bank at another spot, he may perhaps find a stagnant backwater with apparently no movement or life at all and see no prospect for change. An individual encountering the river of life from the narrow perspective of his own particular river bank occasionally may need to call on his eagle nature to lift his range of vision to take in more of the river, to see all the curves and turns and changes. Then he may put his own situation into better perspective, and see other possibilities. We need our eagle natures, especially when we seem caught in a particularly grim bend in the river.

The advice given to us in this part of the myth is particularly appropriate for us today. Almost every woman I know has waded right out into the river and has been overwhelmed. Almost every woman I know is too busy. She is into this, studying that, driving in a carpool to this and to that, working on some charity project, racing around until she is ragged. She needs to be quiet, to approach the vastness of life's responsibilities in a more orderly manner, to do one thing, take one crystal goblet, at a time, concentrate on it, and do it well. Then she may move on to other things.

12

Psyche's fourth task is by far and away the most interesting of all, yet few women ever reach this level of development for it is beyond the range of most people's experience. Whenever I begin talking about this fourth task, I feel all the good earth of solid rationality and reason dissolving under my feet. Yet one must know these things if one is called to the last of Psyche's tasks.

Aphrodite says that Psyche must go into the underworld and obtain from the hand of Persephone herself (who reigns there) a little cask of her own beauty ointment. Psyche again collapses. This time the helper that comes to her aid is not a living being, or even a natural phenomenon. A tower gives her instructions for her underworld journey.

Psyche is to take two coins in her mouth and two pieces of barley bread in her hands. She must refuse to assist a lame donkey driver who will ask her to pick up some sticks. She must pay the ferryman over the river Styx with one of the coins. She must refuse the groping hand of a dying man as he reaches up out of the water. She must refuse to assist three women who are weaving the threads of fate. She is to toss one of the pieces of barley bread to Cerberus, the three-headed dog who guards the entrance to hell, and while the three heads are quarreling over the bread, she is to go in. She is to refuse to eat anything but the simplest food in the underworld. And then she is to repeat the whole process in reverse on her way back.

A woman may not undertake the fourth task unless she has first gathered all the necessary strength from the first three. Almost always one needs a teacher or a guide, and unless one has the strength and courage, it is best not to undertake the fourth task. It is a terrible experience to be stranded part way through the underworld journey. Unless one has the coins, the barley bread and, most important of all, the necessary information gathered from the tower, one should not begin this journey.

First one finds a proper tower, a human construction. The tower is masculine, a construct, a convention, a set of rules, a tradition, a system. Christianity is such a tower of strength and the best one for us Westerners. Excellent examples of such towers are the spiritual exercises of Ignatius of Loyola, the lives of the Saints, the Liturgical Year, and Christian Retreats. Farther from our own culture are the many systems of Yoga, Sufi Mysticism, Zen, and other Oriental towers. In theory it does not matter which tower one chooses, though it is generally best for Westerners to remain with the traditions of their western consciousness. Our own collective unconscious has patterns which are best suited to our western ways.

The first thing that Psyche must learn is to curb her generosity, to say no to the lame man and the dying man (but only for this stage of her growth). I once had the profound experience of counseling a highly intelligent woman during this fourth stage. She nearly lost her way over this issue of feminine generosity, of having to say no to somebody. I often had to do it for her when she couldn't bear to do it herself. Somebody would phone and want something and she couldn't refuse. I had to be her tower and refuse for her. This went on for two years. It is a difficult time for a woman. During this task, an old lame man drops a few sticks and asks for help to get them back on the donkey and she has to say no; or a dying man reaches up and she must say no.

Kindness and gift-giving are very curious virtues. Our Christian attitude toward generosity gives us almost no alternative but to be kind. When I was in India, I found a different attitude toward kindness. When I would think I was being kind to a beggar, for instance, my Indian friend would say to me, "Robert, why do you interfere in other people's lives?" I finally found an answer for him. I said, "Because I need to." "Well," he said, "if that is the case, then it's all right."

We are talking about the creative NO, not an indifferent NO. A woman has to come to a creative, limiting, form-giving NO. A Chinese proverb observes that the man stands on a mountain at sunrise and holds his hands forth, palms up, saying the creative YES. The woman stands on a mountain top and holds her hands forth, palms down, and says the creative NO. It is this creative NO which we are examining here.

This is true for a woman only in this fourth stage, only when she has completed the other tasks. If she has not learned to be generous, this task will be poison to her. There are only certain times when the creative NO is required. Then one drops it and can be generous again.

We do not have the bony hands of beggars in our society, but we have the demands on our time. The phone rings and we are asked to do a variety of things. The doorbell rings and someone wants us to give to some organization or charity. I finally decided this was not the way I wanted to give my money, but it took a lot of courage for me to say to the person at the door, "No, I have my own way."

In most primitive societies, if one does something for another, he is indebted to that person. In Africa, if one saves a man's life and that man commits a crime, the person who saved him is responsible. My Indian friend was constantly questioning me about this. He would say, "Why are you doing that?" I would stutter around with such answers as "Well, it's a good thing to do." or, "He touched my heart." And he would say, "That's no reason."

The myth tells us that a woman must not do good indiscriminately at this point in her life. Collective good, particularly, is forbidden. The reason for this is that the fourth task requires *all* of a person's energy and resources.

Ideally a woman goes through her tasks of individuation one stage at a time, and incorporates the strength from one task, successfully completed, to help in the next. But practically, it doesn't work exactly that way. We get all of them crowded together; all four stages impinge upon us indiscriminately. Possibly one should not even know about the fourth stage until one is actually drawn into it by necessity. Otherwise one might begin to nibble at it, or to enter it a little bit. But there is no little bit to this fourth stage. Dr. Jung was adamant about this. He said, "If you are not going to see analysis through, don't begin." To make that great subterranean journey, the night sea journey, one must be prepared to carry it through. The ferryman needs his toll. One must have a sum of energy, enough energy stored up in advance to see himself across the river Styx and back.

Psyche must also say no to taking part

in the weaving of fate. What woman can resist interfering in the weaving of the fate of the world, especially the superpersonal weaving of her children's lives, which she should not touch. A mother thinks she should guide her children, and in some respects this is true. But in other respects they are not her children; they are life's children. A mother should not stop her own life to take part in the weaving of their fate. She will serve *them* better by attending to her own fate.

So Psyche goes on her journey to the underworld. She was instructed not to eat very much in the underworld, so when Persephone offers her a banquet, Psyche remembers, and refuses. She eats only bread and water. There is a strong suggestion here. In most cultures to eat a meal someplace is to forge permanent ties with that place, or family, or situation. Where one eats, one is somehow committed. That is why a Brahman will never eat in a low-caste house; it would tie him there.

Psyche gets the cask of beauty ointment and comes away, tossing the other barley cake to the dog Cerberus as she quietly slips by. She finds the ferryman again, pays the second coin for her fare, and comes back.

Psyche brings the cask of beauty ointment up to the surface of the earth, past all these trials and difficulties, and then does a curious and foolish thing. She is suddenly overwhelmed by the thought that if this ointment is so precious to Aphrodite, why wouldn't it be good for her? So she opens the casket. Not beauty but a deadly sleep comes out of it and pours over her. Psyche falls to the ground as if dead.

(Let us carry the story on to the end, though we will come back to this point.)

When this happens Eros senses or hears that his beloved is in danger, flies to Psyche, wipes the sleep off her and puts it back into the casket, closes the lid, picks Psyche up and takes her to Olympus. (She would have died if he had not rescued her.) Eros talks with Zeus, who agrees that Psyche shall be made a goddess, to which Aphrodite raises no objections. She is apparently satisfied. The gods all agree, and Eros and Psyche are married. She gives birth to a girl, whom they name Pleasure.

13

How do we interpet Psyche's opening the beauty ointment, especially after all she had accomplished so bravely?

The beauty ointment may be a woman's preoccupation with beauty or attractiveness, with physical desirability. One can see how important this is to women throughout history, now as much as ever. A woman spends much time with her hair and her cosmetics. A man can never understand this.

Our society's obsession with eternal youth is in large part a demand for Persephone's beauty ointment. There are women who have opened the cask and put themselves to sleep, rendered themselves incapable of real relationships through preoccupation with externals. For a woman who is heavily made up is outside relationship. She has on a mask, as every man knows. Sometimes such women are trying to please and rouse their inner Eros in this outer way, but in the process they lose much of their natural feminine grace.

Psyche's sleep is like a final collapse. It is the long-delayed sleep of death that was prescribed for her in the beginning by the oracle, but which Eros delayed by whisking her off into his garden. Psychological death as transformation from one level of development to another is a common symbol in myths and dreams. One dies to the old self, and puts on new life.

In the beginning, Psyche was a lovely innocent, feminine creature. To acquire new growth and new life, she was required by the oracle, and by evolution, to die to her maidenly, perhaps narcissistic, preoccupation with her own beauty, innocence and purity, and to become involved with life's complexities, including her dark and ugly sides and her own potentialities.

Now who could have understood all of this better than Persephone, to whom Psyche was sent for the beauty ointment? The Persephone of mythology was, in the beginning, herself a beautiful and innocent young maiden like Psyche, alive with youth and springtime freshness. She was preoccupied with beauty, and it was this preoccupation that drew her out of her innocence and into her destined role. She became entranced with a beautiful flower, the narcissus, created by Zeus especially for the purpose of luring her away from her friends so that Hades, the god of the underworld, could snatch her up and carry her away to the underworld to be his bride. After the rape of Persephone by Hades, and after her mother Demeter's long search and grief for her, Zeus finally permitted Persephone to come back from the underworld once each year in the spring.

Persephone had learned about beauty, its worth and its cost. She brought it yearly to the earth in the spring and summer, and she saw it wither and die with the first breath of frost as she descended again into the underworld. Yes, she knew about the fragility and desirability of beauty of any kind.

And so it is to Persephone that Psyche is sent in her final task. What better place? To whom else should the beautiful young Psyche be sent when she needed to die to her virgin springtime preoccupation with her own narcissism, her own beauty, the narcissism that separated her from growth and from her fellow men?

Psyche had worked her way through three of the tasks, assimilating in each one progressively a more complex and more thorough-going conscious self-understanding. Finally she faced the task of individuation itself, wholeness, completion. This required the deep descent into the unconscious, into the underworld, and could only be attempted after she had enough control to work at it consciously.

Curious, that having searched out in the depths of her own unconscious the secret of her problems, Psyche should regress to her former consciousness, open the casket, and die a symbolic death. When she attempts to keep and use the beauty ointment, the old consciousness, it becomes death for her.

Yet in this myth, as in most others, the death turns out to be only a sleep. For the animus, in his proper dimensions in the inner world of Olympus, is able to save the ego and arouse her again to new life on a new plane of existence. Ego and animus now have a proper, whole, complete relationship. She is his queen. The fruit of this union for her is joy and ecstasy, wholeness and divinity.

But we are not quite through with Psyche's death-sleep. Perhaps there has to be failure as well as success in order for any life to be whole. What an insufferable person Psyche would have been if she had done everything perfectly without one failure. The failure reminds her that she is human, and it reminds us of the necessity of failure in all growth.

Psyche's sleep reminds one of Christ's sleep of death in the tomb, or of Jonah in the belly of the whale. This is the great sleep, the great death, the great collapse before the final victory.

We all have been trained to think that progress means success. There must, however, also be an opposite. John Sanford frequently speaks about the difference between perfection and completeness. For completeness, including failure, Psyche needed to fail here at the end of her journey. We all have our shadows, which often save us at critical moments.

When Psyche opens the lid of the casket, there is no beauty ointment in it; there is only the sleep of death. Perhaps it is the persona that Psyche has been working with. Beauty is death for her now.

Eros saves Psyche at the end of the myth, so salvation is for her a gift of wholeness which is not earned, but is given by the gods. One may assume that it is Eros who has been strengthening Psyche all the time. It is Eros, as animus, who has appeared as ant, reed, eagle and tower. If one takes this entirely as a woman's story, Eros is a woman's own interior animus who is being strengthened, healed, brought out of his boyish trickster characteristics and made into a mature man worthy of being her mate. This is all done by her labor and by his cooperation. He in turn redeems her.

It is beautiful to find that some seemingly insurmountable problem has quietly worked itself out while one was busy on practical things. There is a Persian story of a young man who went up to the mountains, found a cave and wandered in. He found a pearl of great price in the cave, but it was in the claws of a dragon that was so overwhelming that he knew there was no chance of getting the pearl. He went away sadly, reconciling himself to an ordinary life, which was uninspiring once he had seen the pearl.

He married, had his family, worked, and then, in old age, when his children were gone and he was free again, he said, "Before I die, I will go back and look again at the pearl." He found his way back, looked inside the cave, and there was the pearl, as lovely as ever, but the dragon had shrunk to almost nothing. He picked up the pearl and carried it away. He had been fighting the dragon all of his life in the very practicalities of his daily existence.

The name of Psyche's child when it is born is translated as Pleasure. I have an intuition that it would be better to say joy or ecstasy. When a woman finally reaches her full development and discovers her own goddesshood, she gives birth to an element of pleasure, joy or ecstasy.

I think possibly the crowning achievement of femininity is to be able to bring joy, ecstasy, pleasure into life. A man values a woman so highly because she has just this capacity or power. Men cannot find this ecstasy alone, without the aid of the feminine element, so they find it either in outer woman or in their own inner woman. Joy is a gift from the heart of woman.

It is a woman's supreme privilege and development to be a bringer of joy. In the last of the Ten Ox Herding Pictures, when the man has come to the highest point of development, he puts on ordinary clothes, walks down all the roads and lanes, looking just like everyone else, except that all the trees burst into blossom when he walks by.

I think this is equivalent to an individual woman's final joyful state. She has and she is a beatific vision. The fruit of all her labors is joy and ecstasy.

Suggestions for Further Reading

de Castillejo, Irene C.: KNOWING WOMAN G. P. Putnam's Sons (Hardback); Harper and Row (Paperback)

Grinnell, Robert: ALCHEMY IN A MODERN WOMAN. Spring Publications, Zurich, Switzerland

Harding, M. Esther: THE WAY OF ALL WOMEN. G. P. Putnam's Sons (Hardback); Harper and Row (Paperback)

——————: WOMEN'S MYSTERIES. G. P. Putnam's Sons (Hardback); Bantam Books (Paperback)

Layard, John: THE VIRGIN ARCHETYPE Spring Publications, Zurich, Switzerland

Lewis, C. S.: TILL WE HAVE FACES Wm. B. Eerdmans Publishing Co.

Neumann, Erich: AMOR AND PSYCHE Princeton University Press (Hardback and Paperback)

von Franz, Marie-Louis: PROBLEMS OF THE FEMININE IN FAIRYTALES. Spring Publications, Zurich, Switzerland

Weaver, Rix: THE OLD WISE WOMAN. G. P. Putnam's Sons

The publishers of SHE! also invite your attention to John A. Sanford's splendid new book THE MAN WHO WRESTLED WITH GOD. In this book Sanford continues his attempt to help men and women of our time find greater wholeness and meaning as persons by reading and understanding the Bible in the light of today's psychological insight. This time he turns to stories of the patriarchs—Jacob, Moses, Joseph, Adam and Eve—and uses them to illustrate his idea of *individuation:* that each and every person possesses the capacity for well-rounded person-hood, a capacity that must be realized through a combination of intention, determined wrestling, canny resourcefulness, insight, and the circum-stances and incidents of daily life. In looking both ways he throws abundant light both on the Bible and on the dilemma of modern persons seeking to find their way. This is good material for adult study, provides insights for meditation and sermonizing, and is just plain good reading for almost anybody. Order at $5.95 from Religious Publishing Co., 198 Allendale Road, King of Prussia, Pa. 19406.

We also have Mr. Sanford's essay JESUS, PAUL AND DEPTH PSYCHOLOGY at $1.75.